SPARKY'S STEM GUIDE TO...

DIGGERS

BY KIRSTY HOLMES

THE SECRET BOOK COMPANY

The Secret Book Company
King's Lynn
Norfolk PE30 4LS

Printed in Malaysia.

A catalogue record for this book is available from the British Library.

ISBN: 978-1-78998-060-8

Written by:
Kirsty Holmes

Edited by:
John Wood

Designed by:
Danielle Rippengill

Original idea by Harrison Holmes.

IMAGE CREDITS

All images are courtesy of Shutterstock.com, unless otherwise specified. With thanks to Getty Images, Thinkstock Photo and iStockphoto. Cover – NotionPic, A–R–T, logika600, BiterBig, lukpedclub, Rvector, KostyaTimofeev. Sparky – NotionPic, lukpedclub, Rvector. Peggy – NotionPic. Grid – BiterBig. Construction School – Dmi T. 2 – KostyaTimofeev. 5 – Mascha Tace. 6–11 – KostyaTimofeev. 10 & 11 – hvostik. 12 – KostyaTimofeev. 14 & 15 – intararit. 16 – Krishnadas, Cool Vector Maker. 17 – Butterfly Hunter, NEGOVURA, Benjamin Marin Rubio. 18 & 19 – piscari. 20 – Mascha Tace. 22 – Alex_Murphy, Martial Red, bsd, T VECTOR ICONS. 23 – Dmi T.

CONTENTS

WORDS THAT LOOK LIKE THIS CAN BE FOUND IN THE GLOSSARY ON PAGE 24.

WELCOME TO DRIVING SCHOOL!

My name is Jeremy Sparkplug, but you can call me Sparky. Welcome to the Horses for Courses driving school. Today we will be learning to drive diggers, cranes and lifters. It's **CONSTRUCTION** day!

You'll be learning to drive some of the heaviest and most useful **VEHICLES** around. If you pass your driving test, you'll earn your Golden Horseshoe. So pay attention: it's time to DRIVE!

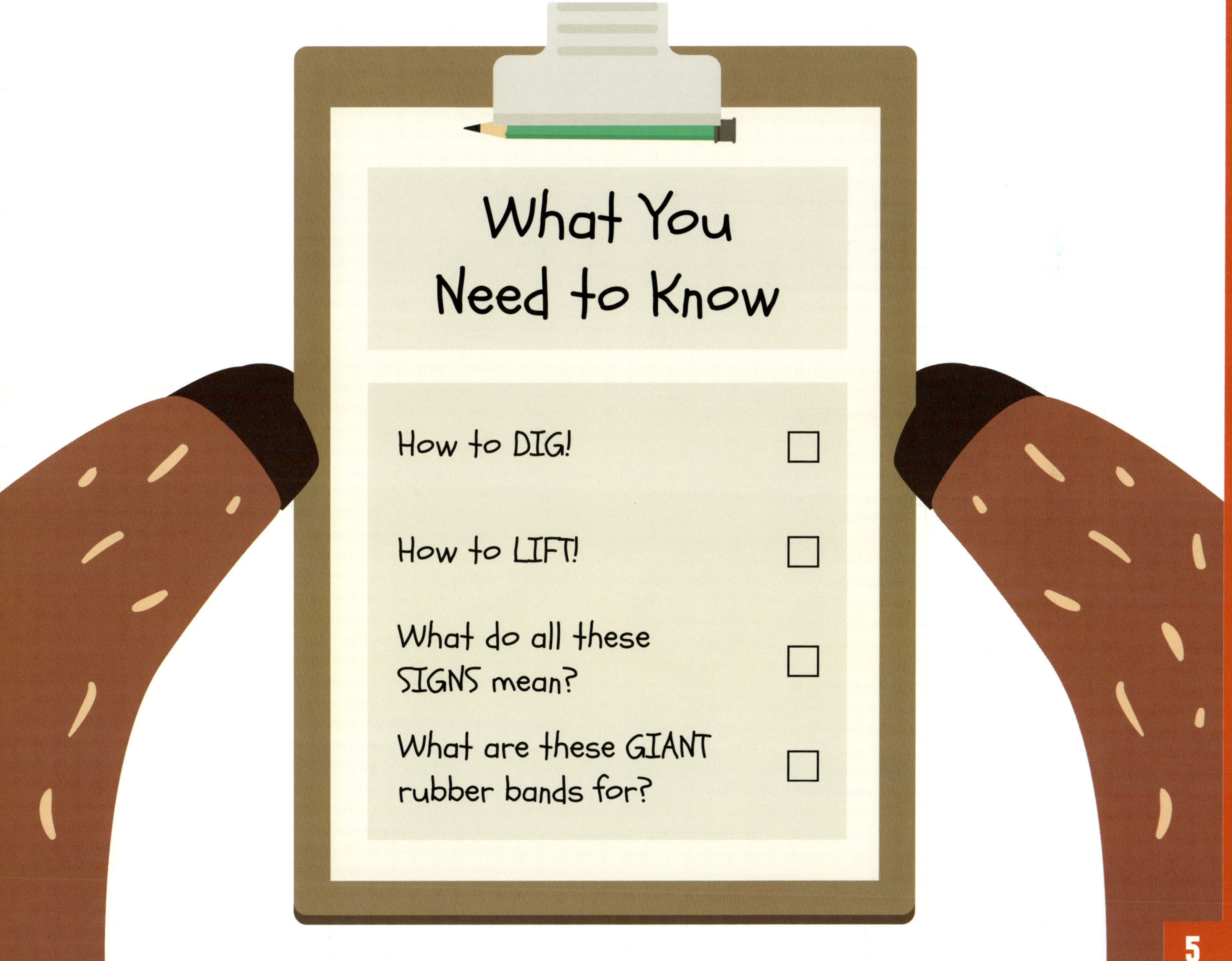

LESSON 1: WHAT IS A DIGGER?

Diggers, cranes, loaders, bulldozers... These mighty machines dig, smash, flatten and build everything around us, from the tallest towers to the roads under our feet. Each piece of **HEAVY MACHINERY** has a special job to do.

HORSES FOR COURSES
SCHOOL
EARN YOUR HORSESHOES
DRILLING RIG
EXCAVATOR
BULLDOZER
This is Peggy. She's a master builder!

LESSON 2:

PARTS OF A DIGGER

This is a digger. Its real name is an excavator.
Its main jobs are digging holes and moving heavy things.

CAB

This is where the driver sits. It is on a **ROTATING** platform.

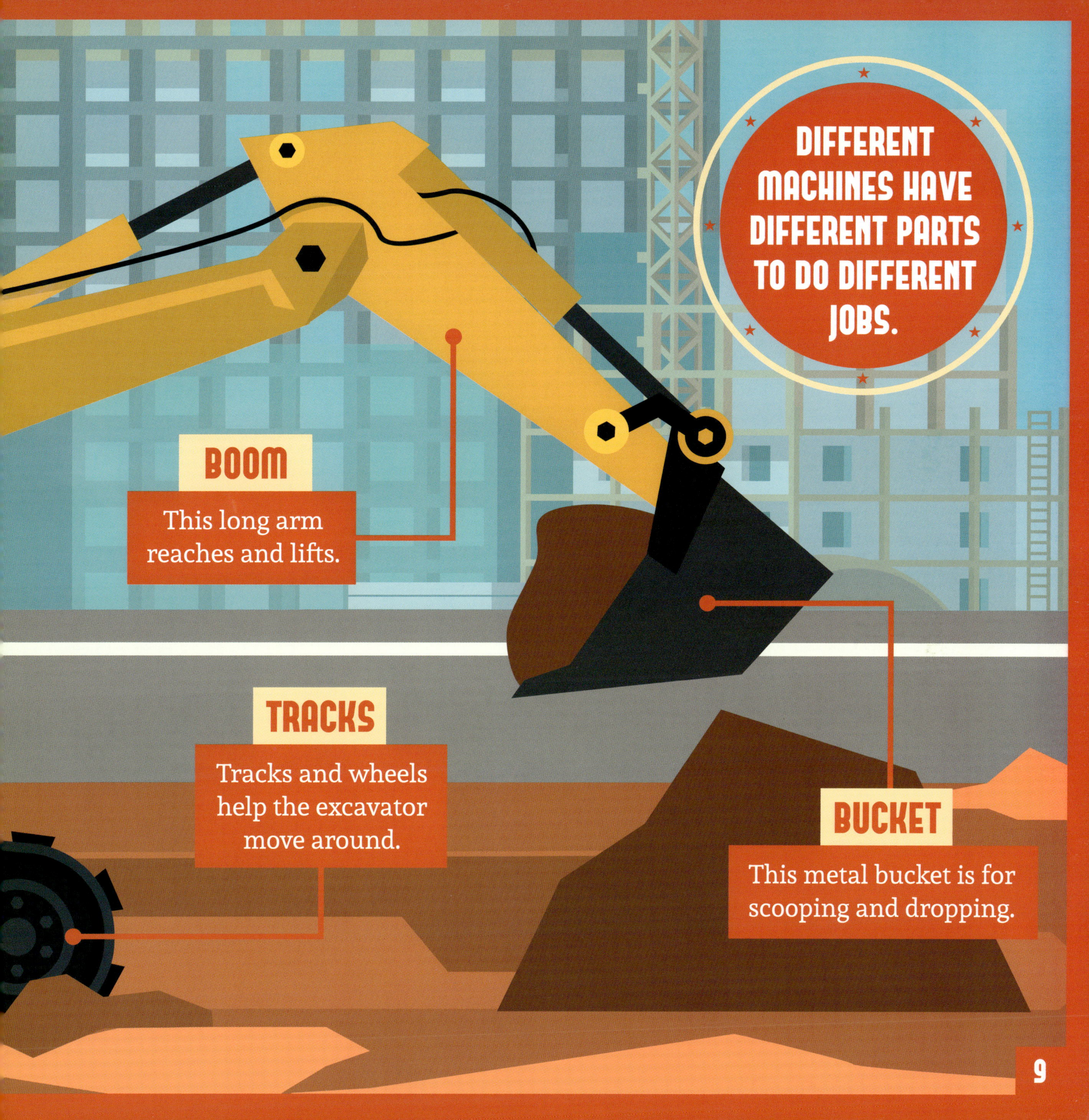
DIFFERENT MACHINES HAVE DIFFERENT PARTS TO DO DIFFERENT JOBS.
BOOM
This long arm reaches and lifts.
TRACKS
Tracks and wheels help the excavator move around.
BUCKET
This metal bucket is for scooping and dropping.

LESSON 3:

DRIVING A DIGGER

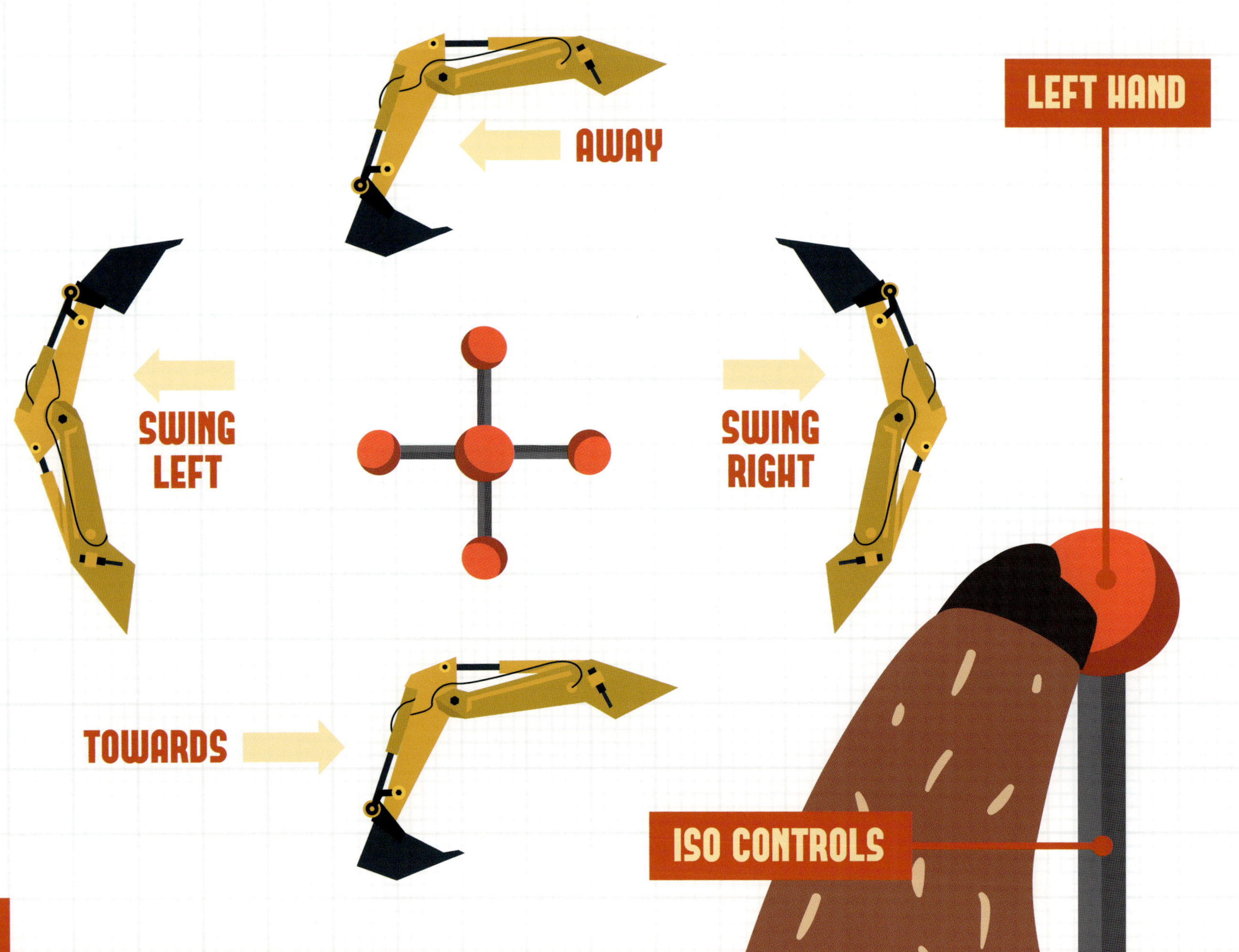

Diggers are controlled using levers and joysticks. The controls on most diggers are the same, so people can drive most diggers without having to learn new controls. In the UK, people use the ISO control pattern. In America, people use SAE controls. These are the same, but the hands are the other way around.

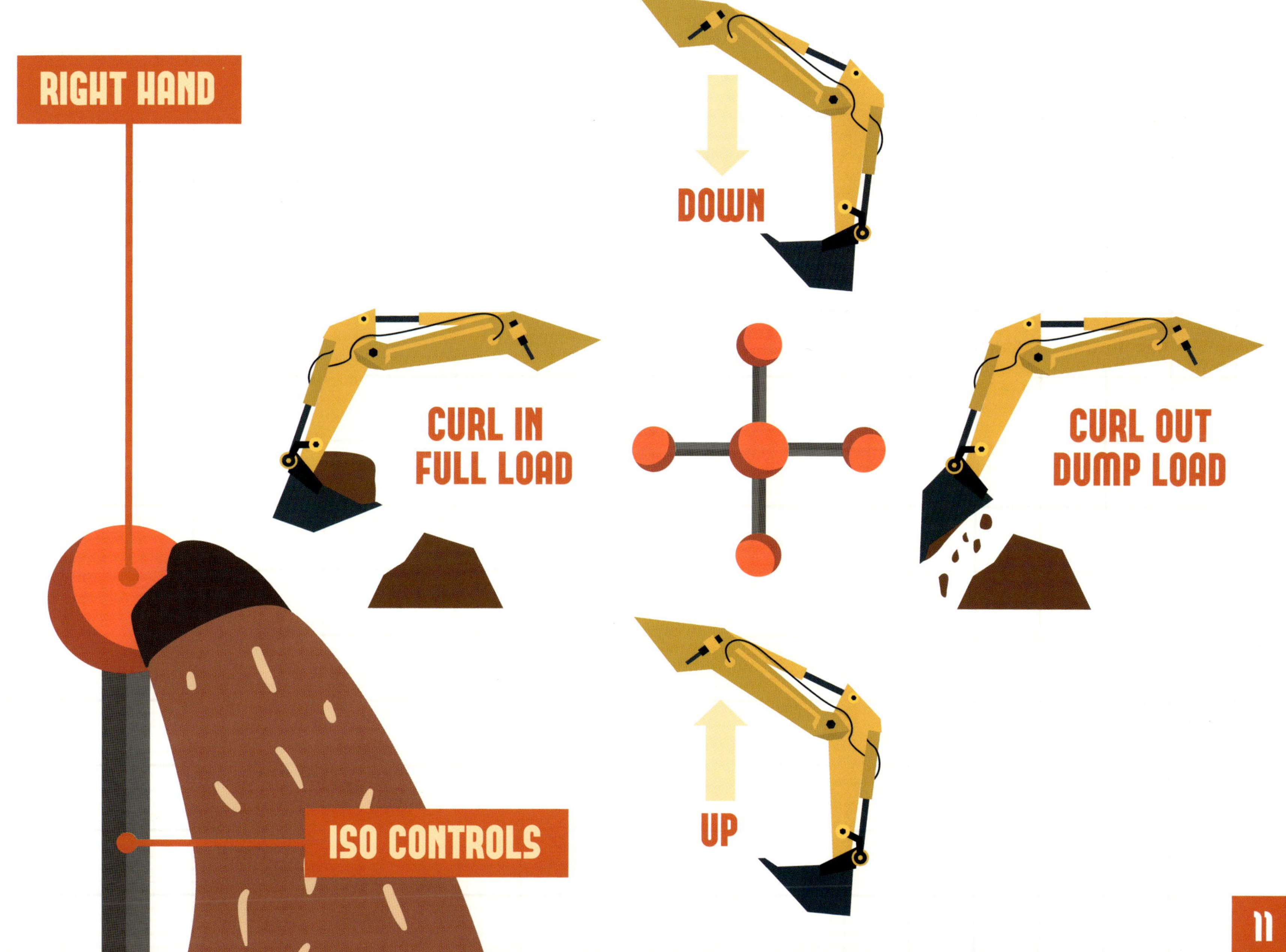

LESSON 4:

DIGGING

Need to dig a big hole, move a big pile of earth, or clear some land so you can build on it? Then you need one of these earth-moving machines.

CHERRY PICKER

These have a platform that can be raised and lowered. Cherry pickers can lift workers or items to high places.

BULLDOZER

A bulldozer is a powerful machine used to push rocks and earth, or knock down buildings and trees. It is like a tractor, but with a big plate on the front.

EXCAVATOR

Excavators can be used to dig, lift, move, crush, clear and **DEMOLISH**.

LESSON 5:

LIFTING

Have you ever looked up at a tall building and wondered how they got the roof on? Lifting machines have the answer...

CRANE

CARGO SHIP

NO JOB TOO BIG...

Cranes are used to lift large, heavy items to high places. Some of the biggest cranes are found at shipyards, where they load and unload huge **CONTAINERS** from ships.

... NO JOB TOO SMALL

Other construction vehicles, such as the forklift truck, can be used to lift smaller loads. This one is loading things into a container, ready to be put on the ship by the crane.

LESSON 6: SITE SAFETY

All these vehicles are really cool. But a construction site is a dangerous place. It is very important that we all look out for these types of signs, which tell us how to stay safe.

YELLOW = DANGER!

Look out for yellow signs, which warn you of dangers.

BLUE = MUST DO

Blue signs tell you things you must do, have or use to stay safe.

FIRST AID
ASSEMBLY POINT
RED = DO NOT!
Red signs mean you must not enter an area, do something or use something shown on the sign.
GREEN = SAFE
Green signs show you where it is safe to go and what it is safe to do.
Remember, everyone. NEVER go on a building site unless you are with an adult...
... and always follow the signs!

LESSON 7:

A BIGGER DIGGER

Some of the biggest vehicles in the world are bucket-wheel excavators. These have a large wheel with buckets on, which turns and scoops earth, coal or other things onto a **CONVEYOR BELT**.

EARN YOUR HORSESHOES

CAN YOU SPOT PEGGY AND SPARKY BY THE BAGGER 288? LOOK REALLY CLOSELY!

BAGGER 288

The biggest of these giants is the Bagger 288. It is around 96 metres tall and weighs 13,500 tonnes. It can dig over 240,000 tonnes of coal each day. It has a top speed of about 9 metres per minute – so it won't break any speed records, but it's amazing at doing its job: DIGGING!

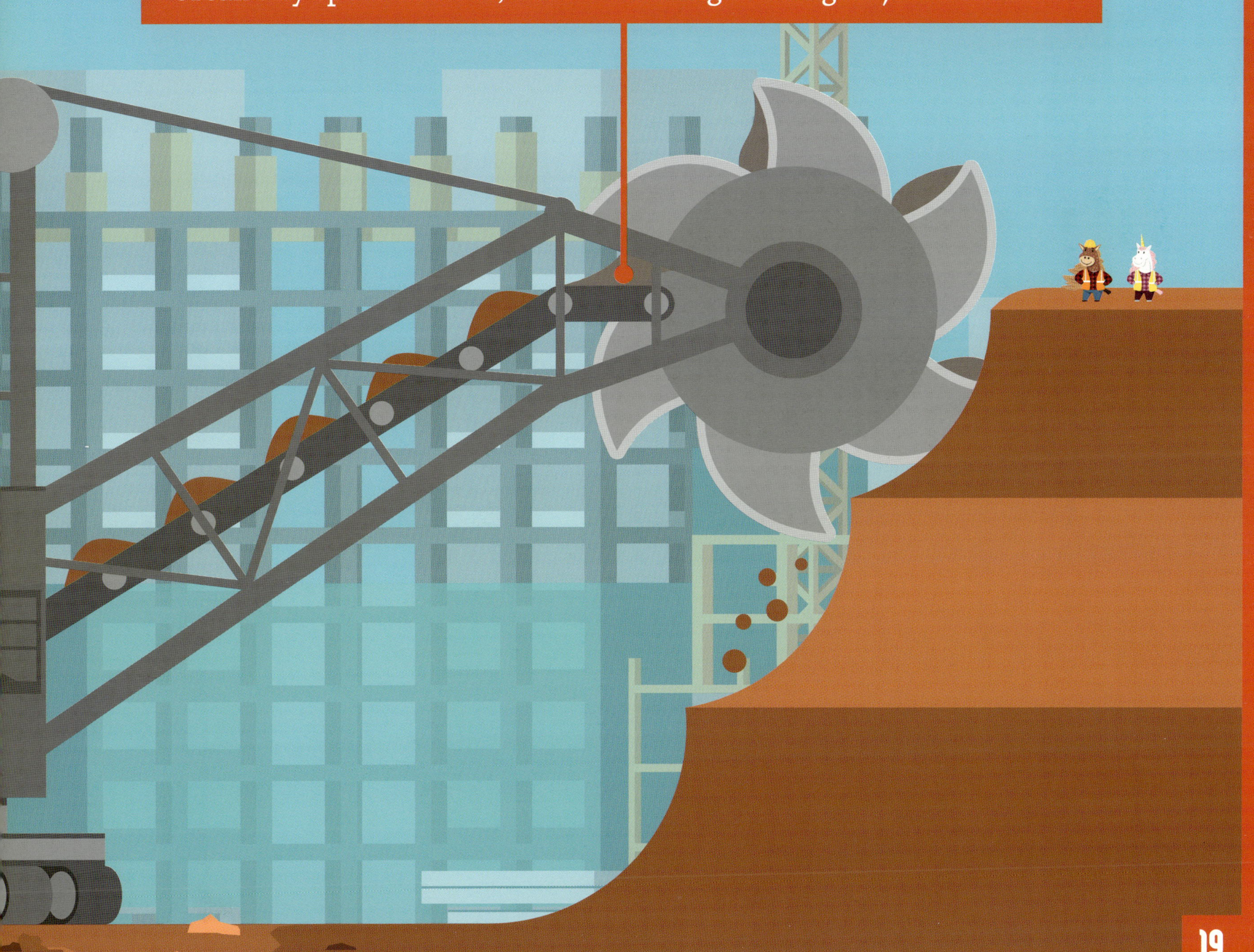

DRIVING TEST

Listen up, crew! You've got to pass your driving test if you want to get your hands on these mean machines!

Questions

1. What does the boom on an excavator do?
2. In the ISO control pattern, how do you curl the bucket outwards?
3. What does a cherry picker do?
4. What do yellow signs mean?
5. How tall is the Bagger 288?

Did you get them all right?

Of course you did – here is your Golden Horseshoe.
Now, do I hear the whistle? Time to get to work!

Answers: 1. Reach and lift 2. Right hand, push right 3. Lifts things high up 4. They warn you of danger 5. About 96 metres tall

Bonus Lesson:

DOUBLE BUNGEE

You mustn't mess about on a building site, and safety is really, really important. However, highly trained, grown-up professionals can use these amazing machines in fun ways...

STEP ONE
Crane

STEP TWO
Rubber bands

STEP THREE
Best friend

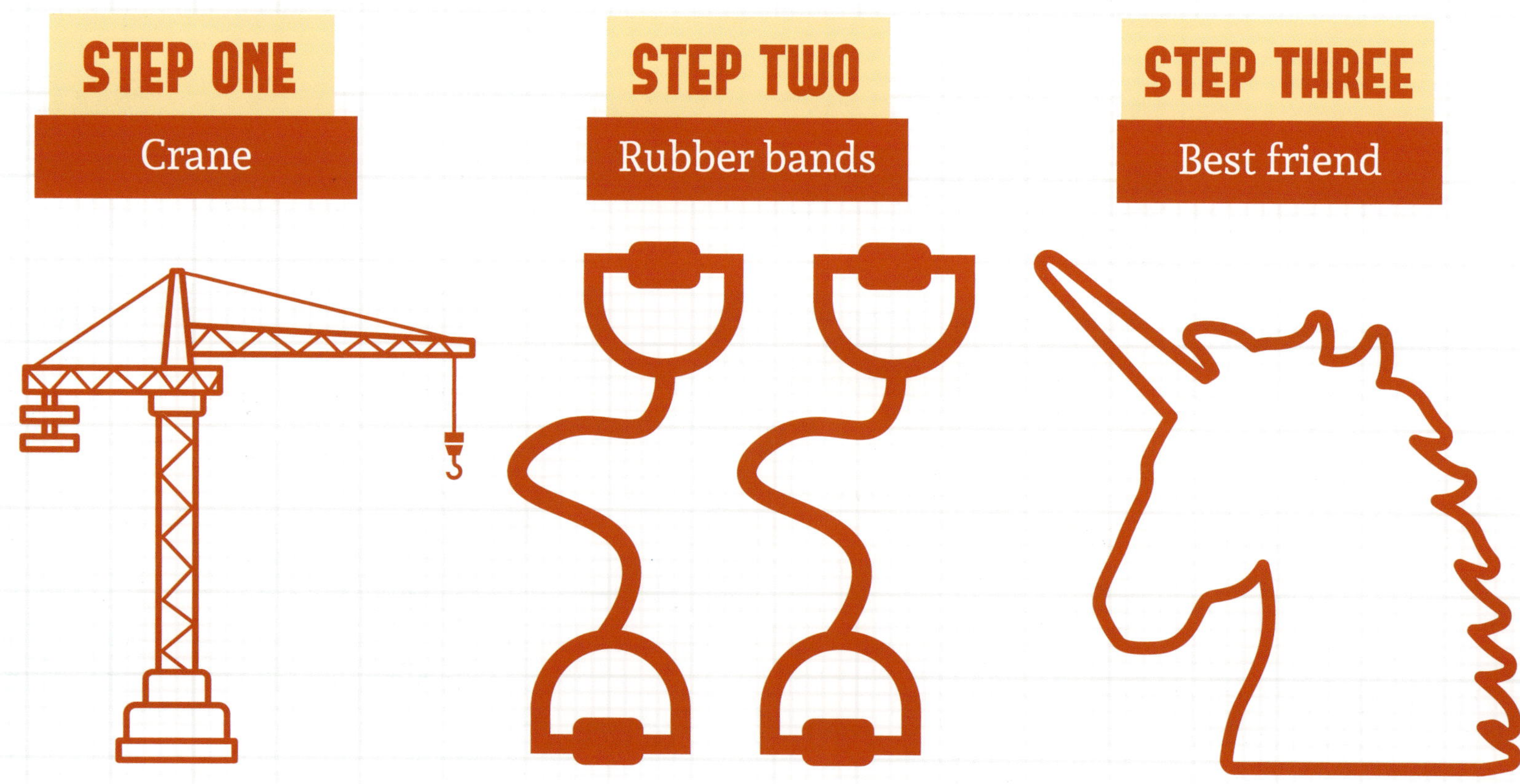

STEP FOUR

DOUBLE BUNGEE!

GLOSSARY

CONSTRUCTION building works, especially related to a building or structure

CONTAINERS large boxes that are used to hold things, which are usually transported on boats, lorries or planes

CONVEYOR BELT a machine with a moving strap that moves things along

DEMOLISH to tear down or destroy something, especially a building

HEAVY MACHINERY heavy-duty vehicles used in construction

ROTATING spinning or turning around a fixed point

VEHICLES machines used for carrying or transporting things or people